I Saw Him

A Journey Into The Secret Places of God

Author: God

Written By: Helen J. Person

ISBN: 978-1-7348501-2-3

DEDICATION

I would like to show my gratitude by dedicating this powerful book to my beloved husband who's an incredible, amazing man. He walks in greatness and integrity. I love you (agape) with my whole heart, Pastor Ronald Person. You have supported and inspired me! There was multiple times I wanted to quit, but with your wisdom and knowledge in the word, you reminded me that it was not me, "…but the Holy Spirit who is inspiring you to keep going until God says it is finished." Ronald, your kind words would keep me going. I would hear you say, "Baby you can do it!" Now that the book is finished, over and over I hear you my husband saying how proud you are of me. I thank God for a praying husband who prayed me through. Thank you babe.

TABLE OF CONTENTS

INTRODUCTION....................i

ACKNOWLEDGMENTS....................iv

1 - UNDERSTANDING DREAMS AND VISIONS....................1

2 - THE DIFFERENCE BETWEEN DREAM AND VISION....................6

3 - WHAT IS OPEN VISIONS AND INNER VISION, TRANCE....................15

4 - GOD GIVES INSTRUCTION THROUGH DREAMS AND VISIONS....................24

5 - GOD WILL TAKE YOU PLACES THROUGH DREAMS AND VISIONS WHERE YOU NEVER BEEN BEFORE....................33

6 - DREAMS AND VISIONS COME FROM GOD....................41

7 - GOD GIVES REVELATION TO UNDERSTAND DREAMS AND VISIONS....................63

8 - NIGHT VISION, OPEN VISION, VISIONS IN A DREAM....................73

ABOUT THE AUTHOR....................130

INTRODUCTION

During my lifetime, I have experienced an extraordinary life with God. I have learned, based on my experience, that God will speak to you through Dreams, Visions, Trances, The Word, Prophets, Prophetesses, and even in an Audible Voice (Isaiah 6:8; Matthew3:17; 1Samuel 3:19). I've heard God's voice many times in the spirit. I am 66 years old and I've heard God speak to me once in his Audible Voice. The sound of God's voice was an extraordinary experience that I will never forget.

I pray this book help you to understand the many ways God speaks to us. He speaks to Saints and Sinners alike, warning them and directing them at times. Think about it. How often do we hear someone say, "I had a dream early this morning"? In 1Cor.1:27, Paul said that "God chose the foolish things of the world to confound the wise." Or in 1Cor. 2:7, "Although many dreams are foolish or senseless to the world, they are precious to those who understand the hidden wisdom from above."

Understanding dreams and visions as messages from God is necessary. When you seek God's counsel and Interpretation about what you saw and heard, you learn truth! He is the interpreter of all dreams and visions, even trances. For example, in Daniel 2:1-48 they needed an interpreter of a dream for King Nebuchadnezzar. They search high and low, but there was no one on earth who could do what the King asked. During the night the secret was revealed to Daniel in a vision. "So Daniel blessed the God of Heaven."

Is there a difference between a dream and a vision? Well normally a vision occurs in the daytime, and a dream occurs at night. "A vision is often like a dream when awake." An open vision for example is when I saw the Shekinah Glory cloud moving. I was sitting in church in Dayton Ohio, during the service I saw Shekinah clouds moving from the front of the church to the back of the church. Later, when Bishop Jeremiah called for a prayer line, as He moved down the line, Bishop Jeremiah stood in front of me and said "I saw it too, first a mist of cloud at the front of the church and then it moved down side the wall and now it's hovering in the back of the sanctuary." The Shekinah Glory is a visible presence of God in the natural world. In contrast, to an open vision, the inner vision is the third eye of the mind and imagination.

The way God communicated with people most frequently in the bible was through dreams. The dreams recorded in the bible often seemed ridiculous, yet their interpretations are quite sensible. For example, in Gen.41:15-27 Pharaoh dreamed of seven cows that ate seven other cows. Then he dreamed of seven ears of corn that ate seven other ears of corn! The interpretation of these two strange dreams saved Egypt from starvation.

ACKNOWLEDGMENTS

I am extremely grateful for and want to express my deepest appreciation to my family, especially my husband for his endless support, and my daughters Danyle and Zerlene Rogers. I also want to recognize my granddaughter Promise Daniel. This project would not have been possible without your help. Thank you, Thank you. First, to my husband who stood by my side the whole time while I was writing my book. When I would ask a question concerning the computer and he didn't know the answer he would suggest I ask my daughters. And they would help as much as they knew how. When they were busy, I could always count on my granddaughter, Promise. She would stop whatever she was doing, to walk me through every step of the way, teaching me how to use my computer. Whenever I called her she made time for me. I can't thank you enough for your labor of love, patience, and generous help.

Sincerely,
Apostle Helen J. Person

1 - UNDERSTANDING DREAMS AND VISIONS

One day on a Saturday evening in 1997, I was sitting in the comfort of my Townhouse Apartments. I had already been fasting for 40 days and 40 nights. I had been in prayer all that day, going from room to room praying. As I walked in the second bedroom late that evening, I fell across the bed with my eyes closed. I dropped into a Trance and saw myself appearing inside of the All Nations church in Columbus Ohio, lying on the pulpit floor. As I looked around, the celling began to open and my spirit (soul) started ascending shortly after through the opening. I looked back and saw my body looking like rags on the floor. I continue my ascent, losing my sense of awareness of this world. Heaven opened up and I appeared face-to-face before Him; I saw the Glory of God! Being in His presence, I had no thought of Earth and no one in it. When I hear people say that your loved ones are looking down or watching over you, I don't believe this is true. The bible says through John's description of heaven that there will be no sorrow there or tears. In Revelation 21:4 the bible says that there will be no illness, no doubt or fear, and no sin. Let us think about this. If your loved ones could look down and see you suffering on Earth there would be sadness, sorrow, and/or pain in heaven, yet the bible said that there are none of those things there. Additionally, why would they go to a better place if the same things that are happening on Earth are happening in Heaven? I was in His presence, face-to-face with Him, nothing else existed or mattered. What I saw was so extraordinary.

I will do my best to explain what I saw. It looked like a pillar of cloud with no defined shape. He had no physical eyes, no physical face, and neither did I. It was like looking in a mirror, looking at me. I remember that there was nothing physical about Him, yet I could see Him and hear Him speak to me. He told me about my commission on Earth, "To teach my people who they are in me, and the power they possess." Then He said, "You must go back now!" I realized that I was looking in the face of an eternal God who is a Spirit!! John 4:24 says "God is a Spirit and they that worship him must worship him in spirit and in truth." I SAW HIM and He saw me. I remember experiencing so much peace being in His presence. It gave me better understanding of His words "Peace I leave with you, my peace I give unto you: not as the world giveth, give I unto you. Let not your heart be troubled, neither let it be afraid." John 14:27. It was like a transformation had taken place. I began to understand and see God's grace in a way I've never quite seen it before. Once I looked in His face, I could see the incredible aspects of God: All-seeing, Faithfulness, Power, Infinity, Wisdom, Universal,

Dictatorial, Unsurpassed, Eternal, Unchangeable, Flawless, and Holy Trinity. Unity of a Father, Son, and Holy Spirit as three persons but one Godhead. He's also like a living personal being who spoke to me face to face as one speaks to a friend.

Again he said, "You must go back!" I said, "NO!!! I don't want to go, I don't want to leave you!!" Then God said to me, "You must go, you're not ready. You've only just begun. I have work for you to do." I didn't know what He was talking about at that time, because I had no remembrance of a place called Earth or Heaven. God continued to speak with me about other things concerning Earth. I could recollect everything that was said and at the same time I began to descend back to Earth. At some point while descending I again became aware of my sense of Earth. I began remembering my daughters and grandchildren and everything else concerning this world. My soul was back in my body which was lying on the floor of the church. Please understand that this was my eternal spirit (soul) ascending before God. My mortal, corrupt, fleshly body remained on Earth. The Bible says in 1Corinthians 1:29, "That no flesh should glory in His presence." It really felt like an out-of-body experience. I saw myself descending from the church pulpit. There were two Pastors, one on each side of me, who helped me up and escorted me off the platform and down the stairs. It took me a minute to collect my thoughts of what just happened and the things I had just witnessed, when upon opening my eyes, I realized I was back in my bedroom lying across the bed. I got up still feeling overwhelmed and fell to my knees in worship.

2 - THE DIFFERENCE BETWEEN DREAM AND VISION

The word trance reminds me of Peter in the bible. In Acts.10:10,11, "…he fell into a trance and saw heaven opened and a certain vessel descending unto him as it had been a great sheet knit at the four corners and let down to the earth." God will speak to us through a trance and give us instructions. The word trance means a state in which you behave as if you were asleep but are still able to hear and understand what is said to you. Trance also means to travel somewhere else in vision or spirit.

God commanded me to tell the people that I have seen the face of Eternal Spirit and He has sent me to teach them who they are in Him. I knew right then my purpose and the ministering gift which I was called to do. In this dream, God gave meanings and instruction, but I wasn't ready to answer the call that had been placed on my life by God. Many years have passed since that encounter. It gave me new understanding of Genesis 1:26-27 which says that the Creator created man in the image and likeness of Himself. So we who are believers are in the same class with God. God is a spirit who cannot die. He is Eternal. That is what makes these topics harder for people to accept. Look at 1 Cor. 2:14, "The natural man does not receive the things of the Spirit of God, for they are foolishness to him; nor can he know them, because they are spiritually discerned." God wants you to know that you are a new man in Him! I am speaking of a NEW CREATED man, the man who has received eternal life into his spirit! The new man that may know the Father's will because the senses have otherwise blinded man's reasoning and faculties. Ephesians.4:17-19. In 1 Peter 2:9 it says that,

"You are a chosen race, a royal priesthood, a holy nation, a people for his own possession, that you may proclaim the excellencies of Him who called you out of darkness into His marvelous light."

Dreams come to Inform, Warn, Inspire, Predict the Future and Present (Prophesy). I'll explain this using a dream that I've repeatedly had before. In thew dream, He was standing in the middle of an archway door, with the most beautiful snowy white garment on and long, flowing, snowy white hair, like nothing you have ever seen on Earth. I've had this experience through many dreams, and I have seen shades of different colors in heaven. What I came to understand is that colors I see when I see God are filled with His Glory. People from everywhere formed a line as they continue to walk towards Him. He would embrace them with so much Love, then they would walk over to a huge rock. At that time I didn't know what they saw. And because of my uncertainty and sense of humanity would only let me go so far. I was afraid of the unknown, so afraid that I would get out of line and leave. But before that, I could see on their faces a big smile with tears of joy in their eyes and a unspeakable glow. The second night I had the same dream I could see the same thing happening. I stood at a distance to watch, still afraid of the unknown. The third night this dream continued, only this time it was a little different. I was standing in line, facing God with His arms open wide, and He was motioning me to come. As I begin to get closer and closer to Him, God reached out to embrace me and the Lord said in an audible voice, "I HAVE BEEN WAITING ON YOU." We began to walk side by side, as the Lord guided me to a huge rock where I saw words on the rock in big capital letters, "NEW JERUSALEM." I was so full of different emotions, all I could do was cry and cry. While being in His presence, it felt like nothing else really seemed to matter. Revelation 21:11 tells us that New Jerusalem will be clothed in God's glory in all its splendor and radiance. The luster of it resembled a rare and most precious jewel, like jasper, shining clear as crystal. There is a spiritual New Jerusalem and a natural Jerusalem. God informed me and explained to me what the New Jerusalem word I saw on that rock meant. It meant that we are New Jerusalem with Him in a city, a collective, not made with man hands. It's a city of life in the center of God's eternal Kingdom. In this Kingdom we have the authority and power to reign forever."

How do we gain access to this eternal Kingdom? Look to Romans 10:9 which says you are born into this kingdom when you, "shalt confess with thy mouth the Lord Jesus, and shalt believe in thine heart that God hath raised him from the dead, thou shalt be saved." New Jerusalem is eternal life, eternal fellowship, joy, light, truth, presence, faithful, and righteous. As the dream continued, I looked to my left and saw a vision of a temple far off in the distance. It was so beautiful, like something far from Earth. It was white with the brightest illuminating light that I have ever seen with my spiritual eyes. Then I heard

God's small still voice speak, because He heard my inner question, "What is that?" He answered, "IT's NEW JERUSALEM!!!!!!!!!!!!" When I came out of it, I realized that it was Spiritual New Jerusalem. I had this same vision once before. In the vision, I looked and saw a temple with such an illuminating light, so bright and lit-up. But this time I could see people, as snowy white shapes, walking around and going in and out of the temple. God is the temple, we are the body of the temple. This was confirmed to me in Revelation 21:22, there will be no temple building in the New Jerusalem because the Father will be there and He and Jesus will be the temple. Out of these dreams and visions about New Jerusalem came a ministry called New Jerusalem Global Ministry.

The focus of New Jerusalem Global Ministry is teaching the people of God who they are in Christ Jesus, and helping them in their transition from the Old Man to the New Man. The Spirit of the Lord is upon me. He has anointed me to continue the

Ministry of Jesus Christ, preaching, teaching, praying for the sick, raising the dead, proclaiming liberty to captives, recovery of sight to the blind, and to set at liberty those who are oppressed. God is speaking about both spiritual and natural things.

The Old Man is ruled by the Sense-mind and the New Man is ruled by the Recreated spirit-mind. The Bible gives us a very graphic picture of the differences between the senses and the spirit. Galatians 5:16 tells us that the Lord says to walk by the spirit, that is the Holy Spirit, that is the recreated spirit and ye shall not fulfill the desires of the senses (sinners being ruled by thought). The Mosaic covenant had to do only with the senses. A senses-ruled mind is not in agreement with the recreated spirit, but the mind has to be renewed. Without this renewal of the mind, there is no real fellowship between the recreated spirit and the mind that is not renewed by the word of God. As mentioned in John 13:34-35, loving one another has to do altogether with our recreated spirits. Now your spirit must govern your senses. Your mind must be so renewed by knowing the word and acting on the word that you can easily conquer your senses. Change your mind, change your world! Change a man's thinking, you change his world! So in other words, everything starts in the mind, with how you think. In Rom. 12:1-2, God is asking that our senses, or in other words our flesh, be turned over to Him. This is because we are so dependent on our senses. All the knowledge we obtain comes through our senses: Hearing, Tasting, Smelling, Seeing, and Feeling.

Depending on solely on our senses can get us into trouble. Let us take a look at the life of Thomas in John 20:24. This gives us a sketch of how the senses-ruled believer might behave. Thomas was a sense knowledge believer. He had to see in order to believe. His senses had to be satisfied. He could not take the word of God independent of his senses.

God knows that we are ruled by our senses and for certain things would not believe, until we can see, feel, hear, and/or taste. This is how the enemy attacks your mind. The enemy comes to destroy your thoughts and hinder your growth through your mind. John.10:10 says, "The thief does not come except to steal, kill, and destroy. I have come that they may have life, and have it to the fullest." But the New Man-you should not be ruled by the senses, but instead be ruled by the recreated spirit. Be ruled by the Spirit of God which dwells in you! We are confronted continually with either unrenewed mind or sense knowledge believers. God, in his great grace, came down into the realm of the senses in the person of Christ. Then Christ arose from the dead and appeared among His disciples to let them see Him, hear Him, and feel Him to appease their senses.

3 - WHAT IS OPEN VISIONS AND INNER VISION, TRANCE

I've come to understand God will take your spirit places through dreams, visions, and even trances where you have never been before. Let me give you another example, another dream that I experienced. I saw myself hanging in mid-air and this one little cherubim came out from within me. Suddenly, others appeared before me and they began to quote Matt.16:18, "Upon this rock I will build my Church; and the gates of hell shall not prevail against it." I heard God saying to me, "I'm sending you to the Hebrews," which I understood to mean the Jewish world.

Another night, while having a dream, this angel came to me in the form of a Jewish man. He had on a gray suit and a Black Yarmulke on his head. We were in a Christian church and he walked up to me and began to say, "God has called you to the nations." I stood silently as he continue to prophesy to me. He continued that I would go to foreign lands and every stick I touched they would be healed. I believed that stick here meant men like in Mark 8:24, "And he looked up, and said, I see men as trees, walking." As the dream progressed, I waited until the door opened. You see, in the Jewish nation there are some Christians that are unwilling or simply choose not to forgive others for their actions like broken promises, emotional pain, or broken trust. We are expected however to make peach, as Psalm 122:6 says, "Pray for the peace of Jerusalem: May they prosper who love you."

I once had a visitation from Evangelist Kathryn Kuhlman after having a long tiresome day. I decided to go to bed early that night. After falling off to sleep, in the middle of the night, I woke up startled by what I saw out of the corner of my eyes. There was a big round circle of light with Ms. Kathryn Kuhlman's face in the center of the circle. She began to prophesy to me about picking up the mantle and starting a Healing Ministry. My thought was, "No one knows my name or who I am. Who would listen to me?" I asked, "Who? Me?" She just smiled with this bright light around her head, and she continue on to say, "He already knows." I received the impression from her that the only difference in what I would do versus what she did is that it was a little different, but she wouldn't enlighten me as to what the difference was. I didn't understand until much later on. God finally revealed the mystery of the prophecy to me. That I would be married, giving me a husband to walk with me side-by-side in ministry, also giving him a wife as a Genesis 2:18 "help meet". In the dream, she next instructed me to stop eating meat. She told me to do this because it is poison to your immune system. So I did just that. For the next five years I didn't eat any meat and I became a vegetarian. But when my body started shutting down and I experienced stomach spasms, after much prayer I had the peace to end my fast from meat. After that season was over, I begin to eat meat again. Around August 1, 2001, I resumed consuming meat, but I limited myself to fish, chicken, and turkey meat only. The next night I was dreaming and again found myself sitting with Ms. Kathryn Kuhlman. We were in her parlor room communicating, having a cup of tea. When we were finish, she walked me to the door and presented me with a set of CD's and tapes. She said, "It's your eternal spirit live."

I have spoken with many people in dreams, visions, and even trances most of whom I have never met in person. I met Pastor Benny Hinn in a dream once. I was at one of his Crusade meetings, sitting in the nose bleed section way up at the top. He began to walk back and forth on this long stage. Pastor Hinn stopped on the left side of the stage and looked up and pointed his finger at me and said, "Hey you come here!!!!" I screamed as I asked, "Who me!!" He answered and said, "Yes you." As I made my way down the long flight of stairs and on my way to the platform we became face to face. He began to ask questions like "What's your mother name?" Then, he proceeded to say, "I WANT YOU ON MY TEAM!!" After that he walked back to the center of the stage and begin to minister to the people. As I left the stage, I looked and saw something I've never seen before. It was such an amazing sight to see. The whole altar was full of waving water. People was running and jumping in the water and screaming that they were healed as they left the altar. The more Pastor Benny Hinn ministered the word of God to the people, the more people continued to run and jump in the waving water. When he stop ministering, the water disappeared. I had not a clue of where it went. People was still at the altar praying and worshiping God. Then I was lead to John.5:1-4, "After this there was a feast of the Jews; and Jesus went up to Jerusalem. Now there is at Jerusalem by the sheep market a pool, which is called in the Hebrew tongue Bethesda, having five porches. In these lay a great multitude of impotent folk, of blind, halt, withered, waiting for the moving of the water. For an angel went down at a certain season into the pool, and troubled the water: whosoever then first after the troubling of the water stepped in was made whole of whatsoever disease he had."

On a Sunday morning at Bishop TD Jakes' church, The Potter House in Dallas Texas I was struck with a vision. In this vision, the altar was full of waving water. I saw sick people, lame people, paralyzed people, people with diseases running to the altar. It kept happening over and over. They continued to run to the altar. As they got up from the altar, they screamed how God had healed them and how free and delivered they were. The altar represented the pool in John 5:4-8, it is the most anointed place in the sanctuary.

Living in the three dimensional world you begin to encounter things you never seen before, such as views of heaven and the visitations of angels. I was call in during a 40-days and 40-night fasted, one of many. I have never willingly went on a fast mind you. I would attempt them but never could seem to complete it. Only when my fast was commissioned by God was I able to make it through. I was lying prostrate, praying in my heavenly language, and I saw in a vision my soul leave my body and be taken to this wonderful place. In this place I saw people working. As I passed by each work station, they would stop and acknowledge my presence by saying these words, "SHE'S HERE!! SHE'S HERE!!!" I soon realized that I was on my way to see the Lord Jesus Christ. As I arrived at my destination, I began lifting my head until my eyes met his eyes. I've seen those piercing eyes once before. In

1986, one night at my mom's house, I was in bed with my head laying on my pillow. I closed my eyes, and before me appeared these two piercing eyes! It startled me so much, my eyes flew open! I couldn't believe what I saw, so I laid down and tried to close them again. The same thing happened! By morning, when I awakened, I started realizing that I had been instantly delivered from one of my main vices. I had a bad habit of smoking reefer, cigarettes, and going out parting. I found myself crying out to God for help. I wanted to stop, no longer allowing this seduction to control me. Since that time in 1986, meeting with those piercing, penetrating eyes, I've had no desire to revisit those bad habits.

In my vision, He stood watching with a fixed smile and a snowy white figure. In all His Glory, I could see Him on the throne, so incredible and huge glowing with light surrounded with a rainbow. It was the most beautiful heavenly rainbow colors I had ever seen, literally sparkling around the Lord's throne. He didn't speak but He knew my every thought. I'm a witness to what John saw as He entered heaven, from the book of Revelation 4.

4 - GOD GIVES INSTRUCTION THROUGH DREAMS AND VISIONS

I have not always made good decisions in my life. I'm not perfect, but my spirit man is. And I don't understand why God would choose me to share His secrets of the spirit world, but I am so grateful He did. God chooses imperfect people to do impossible things! Through my experiences in the spirit world of dreams, vision, and trance, there are times where you might see yourself flying in midair. This has happened to me more times than I can really say. I feel inspired to share my experiences, hoping they will help you understand the messages coming to you from God, and draw you into a closer relationship with Him.

I was sound asleep one night, dreaming, with my arms stretched out screaming the name of Jesus to help me!!!! Suddenly, my body lifted off the ground into midair. It was another out of body experience for me as I could see myself flying. While flying away from danger, over trees and houses and through neighborhoods, in midair a big window appeared before me. I said to myself, "God did It!!" I thought, if it was a manifestation of God, then I can fly through this window. As I moved through the window, the glass window felt like a cool liquid gel on my skin. It was an amazing experience, flying high above everything. I was flying between buildings and through glass doors. There were people there but they couldn't see me. Whenever I sensed danger, I would run screaming, "Jesus help me!!" He would lift me up, every time, high above my enemies. I was reminded of Isaiah 41:10, 12, "Fear not, for I am with you; be not dismayed, for I am your God; I will strengthen you, I will help you, I will uphold you with my righteous right hand. You shall seek those who contend with you, but you shall not find them; those who war against you shall be as nothing at all." Remember Deuteronomy 31:8, "It is the Lord who goes before you. He will be with you; He will not leave you or forsake you. Do not fear or be dismayed."

Late one night while sleeping I begin to dream. I saw myself descending down into a strange place. It looked like a holding cell, which I later interpreted as Hell. I saw men in uniforms, with light blue shirts and blue pants. The stench of evil was all around me!! I could see the darkness and feel the hard core wickedness, tense and poised, ready to attack at any time. It was such a frightening experience being in that type of atmosphere. There was not a friendly face there. I looked around and saw no joy, compassion, empathy, or love! It was darkness everywhere you looked. At first, no one recognized me. All of a sudden, one man sitting there noticed me with them. He quickly recognized that I didn't belong there, so at that moment they all started to rush towards me gritting they teeth. I began to run as fast as I could screaming, " Jesus, HELP ME!!!" My feet started lifting off the floor. But they were so close on me, they were able to start grabbing at my legs and feet trying to overpower me and pulling me down. I kept screaming, "Jesus, HELP ME!!" As I screamed out, they begin to lose their grip and their hold on me because there is power in the name of JESUS! God brought me out of that situation just in time. (As I write this I am screaming in my head, "Won't He do It!!!!") The next night, after falling asleep, I had the same dream. The only difference this time was I saw myself walking in this very dark place. As I continued to walk, I began to see what look like potholes all around me. There were people in every pothole, making strange loud noises, grinding and gritting their teeth, grabbing at one another trying to get out. As I walked along, they were pleading with me to help them. But there was no way out for them. You see at every pothole there was a person with a long fork standing guard jabbing at them to get back. As I proceeded to walk through this place, I was making sure I stayed away from the potholes. Far off I could see out of the corner of my right eye a figure of a man sitting on this big throne and He said, "HELL IS REAL!!" When I opened my eyes, I was back in my bed. God will truly take you places in Him (Spiritually) through dreams, visions, and trances. Places where you never visit before, or ever want to visit again, only to reveal revelation and truth through interpretation from God.

Early one morning while sitting on the couch, my eyes were closed but I was not asleep. I fell into a trance and a door appeared before me. I was aroused with curiosity to see what was on the other side of the door. I walked through the door and closed it behind me. After I closed the door, water began to move all around my feet filling up the room with crystal clear water. I tried to escape, but couldn't get to the door. I realized that I could see and breathe normally. I stopped panicking because there was such a calmness in the water. It was then that I knew it was the Holy Spirit performing a baptism. And when the Holy Spirit had accomplished Its mission successfully, the water in the room begin to recede. My eyes opened and I tried to compose myself by being still, collecting my thoughts and feelings from this marvelous visitation.

I've had this type of encounter before. As I recall, it has happened a couple times!! One night, while in a deep sleep, I was dreaming that I was standing on a beach in the afternoon. The waves in the ocean began to travel toward the shore in a normal wave pattern. Quickly it started to change. I would turn and run from the water each time the waves travelled to shore. I begin to notice each time the waves of water would come in, each wave would be much higher than the last one, until it reached the level of my waist. I noticed how aggressive it became with me. So I looked around and saw that there was a big rock sitting in the water. I told myself to move toward the rock to escape, because the next time the waves came in, they would be over my head. I also realized that there was a voice from the water, trying to get my attention. The voice wanted me to stand still long enough for it to speak to me. I made it out to the safety of the rock. While I was standing on the rock, there appeared before me this large wave. The voice from the water spoke to me with such vigor and power. It said, "If you stretch forth your hand and say 'PEACE BE STILL!!', I will obey!" I listened and followed the instructions provided. I stretched forth my right hand and said, "PEACE BE STILL!!!" to the waters. The ocean waves begin to relax and descend. The power of God's words shown through demonstration in a dream and nature.

After reading in the book of Esther.5:2-4, I had a dream about a man sitting in authority extending to me a golden scepter. The man was saying to me, "Whatever you want It's yours." It was later that I understood what the scepter meant. The scepter was a symbol of Authority with power and grace. A scepter is a rod or staff given to a king or someone in a higher position or an official. Three times this figure of a man (I felt it was Jesus) came and appeared before me extending a rod. He spoke not a word, his only communication to me was with His eyes. His eyes seemed to say, "This belong to you!" I didn't realize at first why Jesus would appear on a mountain tending sheep and extend His rod to me. It was sometime after this dream, after I've been chosen and given the gift of an Apostle, that it all began to make sense.

In a vision, I saw Jesus sitting in the heavenly bleacher with other people dressed in all white. He was waiting to greet each person with a big hug as they walked toward Him in their new body. The Lord said to each one, "I've been waiting on you." These are they that believe. The bible tells us in 2 Corinthians 5: 6-9, "Absent from the body and to be present with the Lord." It was like watching from afar. Then, I saw me in my new body walking toward Jesus with stretched out arms as He ran to embrace me. With love and adoration, I dropped at His feet to worship Him. The Lord said to me, “Don’t do that! Stand up! You’re at Home now!”

5 - GOD WILL TAKE YOU PLACES THROUGH DREAMS AND VISIONS WHERE YOU NEVER BEEN BEFORE

Dream are a method through which God communicates with us. He sends us messages about and through His scripture and His concerns, judgments, and blessings to help us understand His purpose for our lives through our dreams. Romans 8:9 (MEV) says that, "You, however, are not in the flesh but in the Spirit, if indeed the Spirit of God lives in you." In our dreams, God will deliver messages like He did in the bible with Daniel. In Daniel 7, Daniel had symbolic dreams that showed future events for his time and prophetically for our day. Like Daniel of old, God showed me some future events. In 2015, while living in Detroit, Michigan, one night I was feeling very tired. I decided go to bed early and fell into a deep sleep. I started dreaming and in the dream, I could see myself inside the sanctuary. It felt like I was standing outside looking in at the Potter House Church, located in Dallas, Texas. I couldn't believe what I saw. The church was almost empty. Only a few people were around. They were sitting and standing in small groups in different parts of the sanctuary. The praise and worship team was on the platform getting ready to worship. I looked around and saw out the corner of my eye Bishop T.D. Jakes walking into the sanctuary from the back. Bishop sat on the corner of the platform with his head down in disbelief. He opened his mouth to speak to the people in the sanctuary but no one was listening to him. It seemed like they were ignoring him. Bishop proceeded to teach and preach about the gospel of the kingdom of God. As I continued to move about through the sanctuary, the people stop chatting and moving from one group to another and began to settle down and listen to his kingdom message. This vision was a future warning! At that time, I had no way of making contact with the Bishop to warn him.

Let's continue looking at Daniel's experience. Some of the dreams and visions so impacted Daniel, that his spirit grieved for days. Daniel shared one of his symbolic dreams, which revealed the future antichrist system through the symbols of four great beasts coming up from the sea. The Great Sea is the Mediterranean. The first beast was a lion representing Babylon. The second beast, a bear representing Media-Persia. The third beast was revealed in Daniel 7:6. It resembled a leopard with four wings such as a bird would have and four heads. This beast also was given authority to rule. Daniel 7:7 revealed the fourth beast, which was by far the most important and the most frightening. Daniel described it as being very powerful. It had large iron teeth. It crushed and devoured its victims and trampled underfoot whatever was left. It was different from all the former beasts, and it had ten horns. The description continues in Daniel 7:19, "I wished to know the truth about the fourth beast, which was different from all the others, exceedingly dreadful, with its teeth of iron and its nails of bronze, which devoured, broke in pieces, and trampled the residue with its feet; 20 and the ten horns that were on its head, and the other horn which came up, before which three fell, namely, that horn which had eyes and a mouth which spoke pompous words, whose appearance was greater than his fellows." This horn, according Daniel 7:21-22 made war against the saints, and prevailed against them until the Ancient of Days came and pronounced judgment in favor of the saints of the Most High, and the time came for the saints to possess the Kingdom.

Another vision of Daniel that spoke to future events was recorded in Daniel 8:15-16. Daniel, as he was watching the vision, recorded that the one stood beside him was "like a man" but probably was an angel (v.15). Daniel also heard a man's voice instructing Gabriel, the angel standing before him, to give Daniel the interpretation of the dream. This was the first mention of the angel Gabriel in scripture. The encounter with the angel caused Daniel to go into "a deep sleep" but Gabriel raised him to his feet. Gabriel was sent to bring understanding to Daniel's vision.

Another dreamer having encounters with the spiritual was Jacob. Jacob had a wonderful dream in which He saw a ladder extending from Heaven. This suggested the fact of a real, uninterrupted, and close communion between heaven and earth, and in particular between God in His glory and man in His solitude. In His encounter with Nathanael in John 1:51, the Lord Jesus made an apparent reference to this incident and connected it with His second advent and millennial glory. But believers even now can enjoy moment-by-moment fellowship with the Lord. At this time when Jacob's heart was probably filled with regret for the past, loneliness in the present, and uncertainty about the future, God graciously made a covenant with him as He had with Abraham and Isaac. Notice the promises in that covenant in Genesis 28:15: companionship, "I am with you"; safety; "I will keep you wherever you go"; guidance, "and will bring you back to this land"; and a personal guarantee, "I will not leave you until I have done what I have spoken to you."

On the way to Egypt, Jacob stopped the caravan at historic Bethesda to worship the God of his father Isaac. This was a place where God appeared to Abraham in connection with the offering of Isaac. It was also the place where the lord appeared to Isaac. Now He appears to Jacob in the visions of the night, I call this a "night vision" and said, "Jacob, Jacob". And Jacob answered, "HERE AM I." And God said, "I am God, the God of thy father. Fear not to go down into Egypt; for I will bless you and make you a great nation. I will go down with you to Egypt, and I will also surely bring you back again." This was the last of the Lord's seven appearances to him. Notice the personal promise graciously made to Jacob, which would compensate him for the long years of sorrow and mourning for Joseph. God cares for the personal needs of His servants (1 Peter 5:7).

The word of the Lord may also come to us in a vision. I am writing this book in the hopes that it may help you understand your dreams, visions, and trances to draw you into a closer relationship with God. A good example of these visions happens in Acts 16:9-10 where a vision appeared to Paul in the night (another Night Vision as mentioned earlier). The passage reads, "A man of Macedonia stood and pleaded with him saying, Come over to Macedonia and help us. Now after he had seen the vision, immediately we sought to go to Macedonia, concluding that the Lord had called us to preach the gospel to them." Paul was at the right place at the right time to receive the call to go to Macedonia. God never gives a person a vision without revelation in His

Word. Pray about your vision and see if it agrees with scripture.

6 - DREAMS AND VISIONS COME FROM GOD

Dreams and visions come from God and what a perfect way for Him to reveal His will to us. Years ago when I was much younger in my late 20s, I would have visitations from God about preaching the gospel. God is still speaking today through many mechanisms: dreams, visions, trances, audible voice, word, prophets, and prophetesses. A dream is something that occurs when a man is asleep. A vision is something that occurs when a man is awake. God uses our dreams and visions to bring us instructions. It is a perfect time to get our attention.

My second marriage is the perfect example of this. After going through a long difficult divorce in 1987, I begin to remember Habakkuk 2:2, "Write the vision and make it plain." So, I began to write the vision concerning a mate for me. Every morning I would pray for him, even though I had never met him. I started having night visions, about his hands. Also in the visions I could see His small framed body sitting in church. I came to realize that there was a mystery surrounding these visions. I begin to notice in each of the visions the colors of his suits, sometimes brown, other times blue or tan. The mystery was that I could never see his face. As time went on, people I knew begin to stop me and prophesy to me about this mystery man.

While resting at home one night, I had gone to bed early while watching TV. Suddenly falling asleep, sometime later I begin to dream. In the night vision I received, I saw there was a man sitting in a chair at his desk in a small room covered from wall-to-wall with books. The door was open as our eyes met. He started speaking about future things to come such as science. He talked a lot about creation and being created. And before the conversation ended He looked up and said these words, "God heard your prayers! He hadn't forgotten!! It's still coming to pass." I had a strange look on my face as if to say, "What are you talking about." He replied to my look saying, "You know!! About your husband! He still has a husband for you. God knows your heart's desires." This was confirmed for me by Psalm 37:4, "Delight yourself in the Lord, and he will give you the desires of your heart."

One Sunday morning at church, when the service was over, one of the Evangelist on staff approached me. They began to speak these words, from Habakkuk 2:3, "For the vision is yet for an appointed time, but at the end it shall speak, and not lie: though it tarry, wait for it; because it will surely come, it will not tarry." I was so overwhelmed because it was exactly what I needed to hear at that time.

As time went on, one day my friend Jean called me on the phone. She was crying so hysterically, trying to tell me that her mother was dying. I rushed to the hospital to be by her side. Upon my arrival, she wanted to take a cigarette break just to get away and process the situation about her Mom passing away. During that cigarette break, she began to share how much she treasured our friendship then she spoke these words, "God has a Husband for you, I can see him but not his face (this would be an example of an Open Vision). He is a God fearing man who loves you very much. He is a man that knows his responsibility as a husband. Also he's a very special and honest, good looking, man who loves the Lord with all his heart. You're going to be pleased and very happy. You have been through a lot. You have been patiently waiting on God." Then she said, "I know you deserve a good man because you are a good person. Helen, don't worry about anything." I knew it was not her speaking from her knowledge but as a message from

God. When she finished speaking, we went back upstairs and walked in her mother's room. The family had gathered around her mother's bed to say their goodbyes. We had arrived just in time to say good bye to her with a kiss for the very last time and then she died.

Now God really does have a sense of humor. More time passed and I met and started dating this man. Minister Peter Christian, for two years. He was from my church where I was attending at that time. Being in a relationship with him was like riding a roller coaster because of his character and activity. During this relationship, one Saturday afternoon he stopped by for a visit. I heard a knock at the door of my townhouse apartment. We sat in the living room, he was on the sofa and I was sitting in a chair across from him. We were enjoying our conversation, sharing our life experiences in Ministry. Since I had already cooked, I offered him something to eat. "Yes, thank you," he replied. After dinner, we continued our conversation when all of a sudden he started to speak in a very prophetic way (he was likely receiving an Open Vision) about this man and our future together. He spoke in such detail and revelation that after five minutes went by I realized that It was not him speaking on his own. God truly was communicating to and through him. When he was finished speaking, I had some questions. First I asked, "Did you see his face?" He answered, "No." I then asked, "Did you remember anything that you said?" He responded, "No, not everything." I continued, "Did you think this man you spoke about was you?" After a couple of minutes he slowly answered, "Well, yes." I didn't want to hurt his feelings, so I said nothing. Well, not long after that we ended the relationship and went our separate ways in the church.

Doing church service one night, our Assistant Pastor Bob called me up to the front of the church and begin to prophesy (a form of Open Vision) to me about me, a man who God has showed him, and our future together. God will show man visions first then will come the prophetic word. As I begin to listen to the prophecy, I realized that there was a difference in his open vision versus the previous ones I heard that came from other people. God had showed him what the others had not seen, my husband's face! He begin to speak about this man in the past, present, and future tense. He told me that he (my future husband) has experienced a lot of pain due to life decisions made when he was a child and when he became an adult, then from his own decisions. He went on to say that he is a God fearing man and very wise, loves the Lord, but because of what he went through and endured, you must be patient with him. This will be a sign, so you will know he's the one. When he shows up having a salt and pepper mustache and beard then you know that's him. The church exploded with much excitement because they knew at that point, I had been waiting for such a long time, for this, at that time, exactly 27 years. Chasing this vision, along the way God would use different people to prophesy about my husband to be. It would remind me of His Word, "Although it tarry wait for it" (Habakkuk.2:3). No one ever knew about the night visions that came from God or that I too had never seen my future husband's face.

Years had passed, since my Assistant Pastor Bob released that prophetic word. I would like to share with you my reader, about the night vision that came to pass concerning my Husband to be and confirming the word of God.

One day prior to relocating to Arlington Texas from Dayton Ohio, my friend Jean Harrison who lived in Columbus Ohio and I were in a conversation on the phone. During that time, she mentioned that she had a cousin who was single, living in Toledo Ohio, and she asked me would I be interested in meeting him. She went on to share more information about him and due to what she shared with me surprisingly I answered, "No" (in my head I said to myself "It's not time"). We continue to debate about my answer, so we agree to disagree and the conversation came to an end. A whole year passed by. We never mentioned his name again, until one day while talking to her on the phone, I asked her about her cousin, specifically, "How was he doing?" She was still quite upset with me and didn't reply to my question, so I respected her choice. We continued the conversation for over a hour then we ended the call.

As I said earlier, my children and I had moved to Arlington, Texas. Yes, she and I stayed in touch, from time-to-time, talking on the telephone, over the next four years. After being in prayer for my husband to be for many days, weeks, months, and years, I begin to feel a little tired and weary in my enduring to wait. I cried out to God one night from a deep, deep place in my soul. A place I've never been before. Weeks had passed since that particular prayer went before God.

It was weeks more after that, when one day the

telephone rang. It was my friend Jean Harrison! She said, "Hello how are you doing?" I replied, "All is well." She asked me, "Do you remember my cousin, Pastor Ronald D. Person who I wanted you to meet?" I answered, "Yes, I remember him." Well she said, "I've been talking to him about you and now He wants to see a picture of you." Without giving it a second thought, I sent two pictures to her phone, which she forwarded to his phone. I don't know why I never asked to see a picture of him. Within five minutes, my phone was ringing and Jean said, "He saw your picture and he said 'WOW! I want Her phone number!'" He called me the very next day, which was a Friday evening.

We talked and talked and talked for hours that day. I mentioned how consistent his cousin was in trying to bring us together. During our conversation, I mentioned about that delay. He shared with me that for the past four years he was going through some health issues and dealing with the loss of his late wife.

He was hurting at that time and wasn't really trying to meet anyone. The next day, which was Saturday, at 10:00 am he called. I was so happy to hear from him again. As we began to talk, he said, "I have something to tell you." "Ok", I replied, "Tell me!!!" He changed his mind and said, "It can wait." We finished our conversation, but before it ended, I tried to press him one more time to tell me what he wanted to say earlier, but he wanted to wait. It was the third day now, as I was walking in the park talking on the phone with Ronald. He asked if he could come to see me. My answer was No, because I thought it was too soon. After all I had only been speaking with him on the phone for three days. His response was, "OK, I'll wait until you're ready to see me." We continued to communicate every day. A week passed. One day while on the phone with Ronald, I informed him that I would be off the phone for the next three days to pray and talk to God. I wanted to confirm if Ronald was the one that God sent. After the three days were up, we spoke on the phone. Ronald asked me, "So what did the Lord say?" I begin to share what I heard the Lord say to me. This is what the Lord said, "IT'S ME IN HIM LOVING YOU!" over and over I heard these words. GOD IS LOVE! (1 John 4:8)

Marriage is great when God brings two people together by His LOVE! Little did I know what else was in store for me!!! Three weeks later, Ronald informed me that he'll be in Texas that following Wednesday to see me. At first, I was speechless for a minute, finally I said "OK!", because I realized that it was time!!! He couldn't wait any longer. He was a man on a mission who had a plane ticket. Ronald had already purchased his airline tickets, paid for his hotel room, and rented a car. When the plane landed, he called me to let me know he was picking up the rental car, and he would be on his way to see me.

That afternoon my heart was racing so fast from being so nervous, yet at the same time, full of joy. There was a knock at the door about 1:00 p.m. I knew when I opened that door, my whole life was about to change. So, I wasted no time in throwing open the door to meet my husband to be. There he was finally was in the flesh, tall and handsome, wearing a black suit. I was so excited to see him! The first thing I did was look at his hands. I couldn't stop smelling him. I was feeling so emotional and for the first time when I saw his eyes it was like looking in the face of the vision. After all I had only been waiting 27 years for the Vision to come to pass. Remember when God shows you a vision, it might take minutes, days, weeks, and even years, but keep trusting and believing, and don't give up! Surely Ecclesiastes.3:1 sums it up well where it says, "For everything there is a season, and a time for every purpose under Heaven."

That Wednesday was our first date. We did our meet and greet as we embraced (hugged) each other. No kissing on the first date, not one kiss. After that we went to dinner and from dinner, I dropped him off at his hotel. I proceeded home to change clothes and I arrived back at the hotel about 6:30 p.m. to pick him up. Then we went to the Potter House Church for Wednesday night Bible study. When the bible study was over, he dropped me off at home, as he proceeded to the hotel. Ronald was only able to stay from Wednesday till Saturday evening. At that time, he was a Pastor for a Church in Toledo, Ohio called New Birth Christian Fellowship Church.

On our second date which was Thursday, we started out with a walk in the park. From there we went to having breakfast, good conversation, and just laughing and enjoying each other's presence. We did some sightseeing around town. He met my daughters Danyle Rogers and Zerlene Rogers, as well as the grandchildren. It was late and we both were famished, so we decided to go out for dinner. No, we did not kiss on the second date either!

That Friday we had our third date. It started with a walk in the park. Then I prepared breakfast for us, that was my way of showing him that I could cook (you know I had to ladies!). When we finished breakfast, we decided to do a little shopping at the mall. Eventually we stopped for lunch, and later on we enjoyed dinner together in the downtown Dallas area.

Ronald left that Saturday evening. But before he left we had an early dinner on a boat, with the usual great conversation we were coming to expect from each other. Then it was time for Ronald to catch his flight. We finally kissed for the first time, as we departed and said goodbye. In my heart I didn't want Ronald to leave, but I knew he had to go. Thank you Lord, for the time we had together getting to know one another. I found Ronald to be very, very handsome, kind, considerate of others, a giver, very patient, putting others before himself, compassionate, and a true gentleman (a man who held my hand and open doors for me). A man that truly knows his responsibility and his worth as a Man of

God. He was everything that I had asked God for! Habakkuk 2:2 says it all, "Write the vision, and make it plain."

After Ronald left, we FaceTimed each other every day, sometime all-day and night, just laughing and talking! When you're in love, you find things to talk about. Sometimes we would be on the phone until we fell the sleep, still in our clothes, listening to the other person breathing, and when my eyes open there he would be to say, "Good morning!" Three months later, Ronald asked me to come Toledo, Ohio to meet his family and visit his Church. He made all the arrangements including my hotel room. When I arrived in the Detroit, Michigan airport that Friday morning, Pastor Ronald was there to pick me up! From there we went straight to the Great Lake Crossing Outlet Mall. Always a man with a vision, Ronald Person right there in the food court kneeled down on one knee and asked me to marry him. I screamed and said, "YES!!!!!", with tears in my eyes!

The people there were so excited and swelling with such joy for us. We tried to finish eating, but being too excited, we lost our appetite and left the food court. We were in a blissful daze, just walking around the outlet mall, stopping in some of the stores, sharing our newfound joy with everyone we met. We just got engaged!! Everyone was so happy for us. After that, I was introduced to some of his family members like his daughter, Ashantis Person who was at the hotel. Ronald shared the wonderful news with them how he ask me to marry him. They were so happy for us.

That Saturday evening at the family cook-out, I was introduced to some of my fiancé's other family members who were present. Sunday, I was on my way to fellowship with the church family, and meet his mother, Doris Person and his younger daughter, Angel Person. Service was so anointed, Pastor Ronald Person preached a Rhema word, a spoken word of God. Well!! Needless to say, I really enjoy my visit.

Spending time getting acquainted with his family and church members was amazing. That Monday morning, it was time for me to leave and head back to Texas. This time, he didn't want me to go. I felt so sad because I didn't want to go either. Whether we wanted to part company or not, I had to go home. So reluctantly, I got on the plane and I made It home safe. We continued talking every day on FaceTime. Our love was so strong together we became inseparable. Over the next few months, we began to plan our wedding in Vegas for September 26, 2014. It was a joy, watching this vision as it unfolded right before our eyes.

Another example when I was called and chosen sent by God to the Apostleship. Apostleship is one of the Five-Fold ministries gifts (see Ephesians 4:8,11-12). God gifted man to fulfill many different ministries: Apostles, Prophets, Evangelists, Pastors, and Teachers. "For the perfecting of the saints, for the work of the ministry, for the edifying of the body of Christ."

I received a revelation Vision. One night, I saw myself at a praise and worship night service. There was a mighty force of power in the room. My legs were feeling very weak and not being able to continue to stand, when I came to myself I was laying on the floor. I struggled to try and get up. I heard repeated three times a soft, steely voice speaking these words, "PREACH MY WORD!" Initially, I ignored the voice I heard. It was very hard for me to accept at first. It became a fight. Each time I tried to get up off the floor, I was thrown back to the floor. I began to cry. It was not until I responded with a "YES! YES!!" I repeatedly said, "YES!! I will preach your word!!" Only after my yes was I was authorized and able to get up off the floor. In God's time, I received his peace to preach and teach the word of God.

More often than usual my dreams and visions come true. In other words they have instruction, fulfillment, warning, messages, and/or purpose. Well, let's go little deeper explaining about dreams, visions, and trances. One day while working in the nursing home center in the housekeeping department, there was a patient that fell dead, lying on the floor. I heard the voice of God saying, "Go to her." So, I started walking towards where she was lying on the floor. There were doctors and nurses all around her and she had stopped breathing. I stood as close as I could without bringing any attention to myself. I spoke the words of Psalm. 118:17 "She shall not die, but live, and declare the works of the Lord." After obeying the voice of the Lord, her soul came back in her body and she got up. The second time while still working in the same nursing home, God spoke to me again. There was a patient in her room taking a nap who was experiencing health issues. The doctor had called, "Code Blue!!" God said, "Go stand in the doorway of her room," and being obedient to God I moved quickly to her doorway and spoke these words, "I command you to LIVE in the name of Jesus Christ!!"

I quietly walked away. No one ever saw me. Later, I met one of the nurses-aides outside that patient's door. I stopped and asked, "What happened?" She replied by saying, "We don't know. She had completely stop breathing and then all of a sudden, she began breathing again. On top of which, every problem she was experiencing disappeared as though nothing ever happened." I looked in her room, and saw her sitting up in the bed, laughing and talking with the nurses. I realized God had used me in a prophetic way. As an Apostle, I came to understand that God will use you in the fivefold ministry at any given time He chooses to use you. I begin to have more dreams, visions and prophetic experiences.

As the Apostle Peter explained in his sermon recorded in Acts 2 dreams, visions, and prophecy are primary signs of the last days and the outpouring of the Holy Spirit. As we are obviously getting closer to the end of this age, these are becoming increasingly common in our time.

7 - GOD GIVES REVELATION TO UNDERSTAND DREAMS AND VISIONS

I have been given the gift to understand dreams and visions like in Daniel chapter 2 where God gives revelation to understand Dreams and Visions. Dreams occur during sleep. Everyone dreams but not everyone has visions. During sleep, the body's heart rate and breathing becomes slower, and your body temperature drops. Blood pressure drops, muscles are relaxed, blood supply to muscles increases, providing energy to both brain and body. The brain is active and dreams occur and sometimes visions.

I was in a deep sleep one night and began to dream.

What I saw was very disturbing. While standing on the grounds of the church where I attended, under my feet the ground was crumbling. As it broke, it extended around the whole building. There was some construction workers and members of the church that were there. One of the sisters of the church looked at and approached me. I asked her what was going on over there and she responded by whispering in my ear, "BREAKING STONY GROUND." I received the spiritual interpretation of that to be Jeremiah 4:3, "And do not sow among thorns. Circumcise yourselves to the Lord., circumcise your hearts, you men of Judah and people of Jerusalem." I also received Hosea 10:12, "Sow for yourselves righteousness, reap the fruit of unfailing Love, for it is time to seek the Lord, until He comes and showers righteousness on you." It is land that could be productive, but for whatever reason has not been broken up, tilled, plowed, and prepared for planting. The prophets speaking the Word of the Lord are commanding the people to break up that land spiritually! To plow the plowable land that they have. The very next day on Tuesday morning, I called the senior Pastor of the church and begin to share with him about the dream. When I finished, he began to share his confirmation of the message with me. He said, "My wife and I have been negotiating about some property on the west side of town in Dayton to build a new church. Only God could reveal this to you." He continued the conversation saying, "I've already sent some deacons out on the property to inspect the ground." On that following Sunday, Pastor shared the plan with the congregation.

When does a dream become a vision? God used visions in the old testament to reveal his plan. So if a dream then reveals the plans of God, it becomes a vision. For example, the Lord spoke to Abraham in a vision and said to him, "Do not be afraid, for I will protect you, and your reward will be great." But Abraham replied, "O Sovereign Lord, what good are all your blessings when I don't even have a son? Since you've given me no children Eliezer of Damascus, a servant in my household, will inherit all my wealth. You have given me no descendants of my own, so one of my servants will be my heir." Then the Lord said to him, "No, your servant will not be your heir, for you will have a son of your own who will be your heir." Then the Lord took Abraham outside and said to him, "Look up into the sky and count the stars if you can. That's how many descendants you will have!" And Abraham believed the Lord, and the Lord counted him as righteous because of his faith (Genesis 15:1).

Now at this time God changed Abram name to Abraham (Genesis 17:5) and Sarai to Sarah (Genesis 17:15). When God changed a person's name and gave them a new name, it was usually to establish a new identity. (Genesis 20:2-7). Abraham introduced his wife, Sarah, who was so beautiful that when Abraham came into a new area he occasionally feared that the local ruler would kill him and take Sarah for himself.

To protect himself Abraham began introducing Sarah by saying, "She is my sister." So King Abimelech of Gerard sent for Sarah and had her brought to him at his palace. But that night, God came to Abimelech in a dream and told him, "You are a dead man, for that woman you have taken is already married!" But Abimelech had not slept with her yet, so he said, "Lord, will you destroy an innocent nation? Didn't Abraham tell me, 'She is my sister?' And she herself said, 'Yes, he is my brother.' I acted in complete innocence! My hands are clean." In the dream God responded, "Yes, I know you are innocent. That's why I kept you from sinning against me, and why I did not let you touch her. Now return the woman to her husband, and he will pray for you, for he is a prophet. Then you will live. But if you don't return her to him, you can be sure that you and all your people will die."

Two years later, Pharaoh dreamed that he was standing on the bank of the Nile River. In his dream he saw seven fat, healthy cows come up out of the river and begin grazing in the marsh grass. Then he saw seven more cows come up behind them from the Nile, but these were scrawny and thin. These cows stood beside the fat cows on the riverbank. Then the scrawny, thin cows ate the seven healthy, fat cows! At this point in the dream, Pharaoh woke up. But he fell asleep again and had a second dream. This time he saw seven heads of grain, plump and beautiful, growing on a single stalk. Then seven more heads of grain appeared, but these were shriveled and withered by the east wind. And these thin heads swallowed up the seven plump, well-formed heads! Then Pharaoh woke up again and realized it was a dream. The next morning Pharaoh was very disturbed by the dream. So he called for all the magicians and wise men of Egypt. When Pharaoh told them his dream, not one of them could tell him what his dreams meant. Finally, the king's chief cup-bearer spoke up saying, "Today I have been reminded of my failure." He told Pharaoh, "Some time ago, you were angry with the chief baker and me, and you imprisoned us in the palace of the captain of the guard. One night the chief baker and I each had a dream, and each dream had its own meaning. There was a young Hebrew man with us in the prison who was a slave of the captain of the guard. We told him our dreams, and he told us what each of our dreams meant. And everything happened just as he had predicted. I was restored to my position as cup-bearer, and the chief baker was executed and impaled on a pole."

Pharaoh sent for Joseph at once, and he was quickly brought from the prison. After he shaved and changed his clothes, he went in and stood before Pharaoh. Then Pharaoh said to Joseph, "I had a dream last night, and no one here can tell me what it means. But I have heard that when you hear about a dream you can interpret it." "It is beyond my power to do this," Joseph replied, "but God can tell you what it means and set you at ease."

So Pharaoh told Joseph his dreams. I was standing on the bank of the Nile River, and I saw seven fat, healthy cows come up out of the river and begin grazing in the marsh grass. But then I saw seven sick-looking cows. scrawny and thin, come up after them. I've never seen such sorry-looking animals in all the land of Egypt. These thin, scrawny cows ate the seven fat cows. But afterward you wouldn't have known it, for they were still as thin and scrawny as before! Then I woke up. Then I fell asleep again, and I had another dream. This time I saw seven heads of grain, full and beautiful, growing on a single stalk. Then seven more heads of grain appeared, but these were blighted, shriveled, and withered by the east wind. And the shriveled heads swallowed the seven healthy heads.

Pharoah said, "I told these dreams to the magicians, but no one could tell me what they mean." Joseph responded, "Both of Pharaoh's dreams mean the same thing. God is telling Pharaoh in advance what he is about to do. The seven healthy heads of grain both represent seven years of prosperity. The seven thin, scrawny cows that came up later and the seven thin heads of grain, withered by the east wind, represent seven years of famine. This will happen just as I have described it, for God has revealed to Pharaoh in advance what he is about to do. The next seven years will be a period of great prosperity throughout the land of Egypt. But afterward there will be seven years of famine so great that all the prosperity will be forgotten in Egypt. Famine will destroy the land. This famine will be so seven that even the memory of the good years will be erased. As for having two similar dreams, It means that these events have been decreed by God, and he will soon make them happen. Therefore, Pharaoh should find an intelligent and wise man and put him in charge of the entire land of Egypt. Then Pharaoh should appoint supervisors over the land and let them collect one-fifth of all the crops during the seven good years. Have them gather all the food produced in the good years that are just ahead and bring it to Pharaoh's storehouses. Store it away, and guard it so there will be food in the cities. That way there will be enough to eat when the seven years of famine come to the land of Egypt. Otherwise this famine will destroy the land." As you can see in the word of God, He demonstrates how He spoke to men through dreams, visions, and sometimes through trance.

8 - NIGHT VISION, OPEN VISION, VISIONS IN A DREAM

On a cold dreary night while sleeping in bed, I was woken by a touch on my foot. As my eyes opened, I looked and saw a man standing at the foot of my bed with a long, white flowing robe. The touch felt so real. The man standing at the end of the bed begin to speak, "Don't be afraid." The moment I heard his voice I knew who He was. I felt so much peace. It was Jesus! Even in a dream you will know Jesus' voice. "And a stranger will they not follow, but will flee from him, for they know not the voice of strangers." (John 10:5). All of a sudden, my body was being lifted from my bed. Jesus spoke again, "Follow me." As I followed Jesus into the spiritual unknown, I began to see beautiful glistening green grass and green trees. The tree limbs were waving back-and-forth from the slight breeze in the air and tall buildings like mansions were rising up around them. Oh what an extraordinary sight!! As I walked through the door, I saw these beautiful large paintings hanging on the wall. The painting were done with different shades of vibrant and glorious colors, such as Purple, Gold, White, Pink, Yellow, and more. I noticed that there was old style furniture, such as chairs, sofa, tables, lamps, etc., with such a heavenly glow. The floors of the mansions were a black marble. When I made it to the kitchen, there was chefs preparing food. Even the food had a glistening look and everything was free. The taste of the food was indescribable!! As I made my way down the hall, I noticed on each side there were rooms. As many entered the different rooms, I saw old antique Iron beds, comforters with diamonds and pearls entwined in the material of the bedding, it was so unusual. There sitting in the corner of the bedroom was a rocking chair with a blanket thrown across the back of the chair. The whole room was glowing with a snowy white color. As I continue walking down the hall, I noticed another open door. To my surprise, it was another bedroom, filled with glowing bright lavender and white colors. The comforter spread on the bed also had pearls and diamonds going through it. I realized each room had a different color scheme. Gazing over the mansions, realizing how huge they were, I couldn't imagine trying to measure each building. People were everywhere, coming and going in and out of the mansions. I knew who they were, because I could see such a Heavenly glow all around them.

When I woke up that morning, I remembered everything I saw and heard. Since that first visit in the unknown spiritual world through dreams, visions and trances, where I saw these mansions, I have returned at least two other times. Each time, I saw something different that I didn't see before. When visiting this heavenly realm, ever present in the back of my mind was how I didn't want to come back ever to the earthly plane. At that time, I realized everything glows in heaven because of God's presence. When leaving one of the mansions, I met a friend who name was Sueann Davis. I remember chatting with her about what she was about to see and experience. I also shared how good the food tasted and how beautiful it looked inside. As we departed I said to her, "Enjoy, my friend, Enjoy!" I remember going one last time. I knew God would be there because I could smell his scent!!!!! In my own life experience, I've smelt the fragrance of God scent a few times. During my personal time with God, whether it be in my bedroom, car, or church. Just like He is no respecter of persons, He is no respecter of places either. He will meet you where you are. When you're in God's presence, sometimes it smells like a sweet smelling fragrance or like a fresh garden of flowers. God's name is like a perfume or a very soft scent.

As I said, I've experienced the Fragrance of God a few times, as I was in the Lord's presence. Enter into your Savior's secret place through deep worship and prayer. Have a willingness to yield to God every movement and every sound even that of your heartbeat. When this happens, you begin to even smell God's fragrance. "Let Him kiss me with the kisses of his mouth: For thy love is better than wine. His name smell like fragrance. Because of the savour of thy good ointments thy name is as ointment poured forth, therefore do the virgins love thee." Now you are in the secret place. You should begin to smell the anointed ointment in your midst. "Draw me, we will run after thee: the king hath brought me into his chambers: we will be glad and rejoice in thee, we will remember thy love more than wine: the upright love thee." (Song of Solomon 1:2-4). These were supernatural experiences.

Dreams can be interpreted with manifestations. These are more of my experiences during a dream. I am 65 years old and God has been my interpreter. I have lived long enough to see many of my dreams come to pass, over and over again. Remember any keywords in your dreams! Wait on God to interpret them. Here are some examples of interpretations I have received over the years.

A dream about money covered in blood. Money represents your finances, personal values, and feelings of security. Blood represents energy and strength. When you dream and see silvered coins or coins in general, such as quarters, nickels, dimes, pennies, something bad is going to happen. But when you see green dollars or bills, something good is about to happen.

When you are dreaming about muddy water, it's not good. But when you see clear water, it means something good is about to happen. My experience with this message was early one morning I walking around downstairs. I laid my head down on the arm of the sofa. Immediately I was in a vision of walking towards a door. I begin to feel very nervous not knowing what was behind the door. I had received this vision more than one time before and had stopped short of opening the door each time. I decided this time to open the door and go through. The room I found myself in was empty. All of a sudden water started to circling around my feet filling the whole room. At first I panicked out of fear and not understanding what was happening at that time. But I realized the water was not there to hurt me. It was there to Purify, Wash, and Cleanse me. My eyes were open and I could see the water being so clean. I moved around in the water with such peace, no longer afraid. The water started to descend. When walking out the room, I opened my physical eyes suddenly realizing I was still laying on the sofa. It was a spiritual cleansing of me performed by the Holy Spirit!

Dreaming about a vehicle could mean you have low confidence.

Dreaming about being trapped in a small place can represent being worried about the unknown, especially in areas such as Relationship, Ministry, or place of worship (Church). It can express a desire to change your current situation.

Dreaming about a dog represents that an enemy is near. If you are dreaming about dogs or a dog growling at you, trying to bite you, or charging at you in an aggressive way, then this means in reality there is an enemy in your life. It could be someone known or unknown to you, like a pretending friend or a family member. Most of the time it is always someone you know, who you shared your personal experiences with, as you would a close sister or brother. You have no idea who would allow the enemy to use them to attack you. Remember people change. Who you knew yesterday might not be the person they are today.

If you see a person's naked body in your dream, it represents the death Angel or destroying angel, engaging someone near or far. For example, early on a Monday morning after my devotion time with the Lord, I was leaving the office where I was to go back to bed. Falling into a deep sleep, I began to dream and in the dream I saw and heard my husband get up on his side of the bed. As he got up he said, "Goodbye Babe," as he proceeded towards the bathroom door. He fell down and when I made it to him he was already dead. I woke up crying, checking on my husband to see if was he ok. He was sound asleep. I asked the Lord what did the dream mean. It turned out that was this about my father-in law who at that time in the hospital due to the COVID-19 virus. Prior to this dream, we had received good news that Dad was getting better. God didn't answer me right away. He answered on the next day, that Tuesday, when we got the phone call Dad had passed. I knew then that the dream was about his passing.

What does the bible say about the angel of death? "For the Lord will pass through to smite the Egyptians; and when He sees the blood on the two doorposts, the Lord will pass over the door and will not allow the destroyer to come in to your houses to smite you." (Exodus 12:23). "Then it happened that night that the angel of the Lord went out and struck 185,000 in the camp of the Assyrians; and when men rose early in the morning, behold, all of them were dead." (2 Kings 19:35). "Then death and Hades were thrown into the lake of fire This is the second death, the lake of fire." (Revelation 20:14). "And another, a red horse, went out; and to him who sat on it, it was granted to take peace from the earth, and that men would slay one another, and a great sword was given to him." (Revelation 6:4). "Now the poor man died and was carried away by the angels to Abraham's bosom; and the rich man also died and was buried." (Luke 16:22). "Now it came about at midnight that the Lord struck all the firstborn of Pharaoh who sat on his throne to the firstborn of the captive who was in the dungeon, and all he firstborn of cattle." (Exodus 12:29). "So the Lord sent a pestilence upon Israel from the morning until the appointed time, and seventy thousand men of the people from Dan to Beersheba died." "When the Angel stretched out his hand toward Jerusalem to destroy it. The Lord relented from the calamity and said to the angel, 'Relax your hand!'" "The Angel Of The Lord was by the threshing floor of Araunah the Jebusite"

Whenever I dream of fish or catching a fish, someone in my family, or someone connected to the family is pregnant. If I dream of a baby or babies someone I know is pregnant. One night while sleeping in my bed, I begin to dream. During the dream, I was craving fish. I couldn't get enough of wanting to eat more fish. It was the only thing I wanted to eat. As we searched for such a place, we came upon a restaurant that served all you can eat. You already know what I ordered! YES!!! Fish! The hostess seated us and the waitress greeted us. She asked, "Is everyone ready to order or do you need more time to look over the menu?" I was the first one to shout out, "I'm ready to order, I know what I want!" So she took my order and left to give everyone else time to look over the menu, as she suggested. When she came back, the rest of the table was ready to place their orders. While sitting there waiting, I heard the voice of the Lord say to me, "You are pregnant." The craving was so strong and the fish was so good, I didn't pay any attention to the voice or what I just heard. After we finished eating dinner, we were still sitting there drinking a cup of coffee. I was being entertained by the thoughts of the words of what I heard earlier during dinner, when the Lord said in an audible voice, "YOU ARE PREGNANT." Waking up that morning I was remembering what the Lord had said. The very next month, which was the eighth month of the year 1977, I missed my menstrual cycle. I thought nothing of it at that time. After two more months of missing my period again, I became very concerned. I needed to call the doctor and make an appointment, which I did. After arriving at the doctor's office, I was sitting in the examining room waiting for the doctor to come in. When he entered, he began to ask me some questions, and he ultimately gave me a cup and sent me to the bathroom. After making it back to the exam room, the doctor came back in the room and said, "Yes, you are pregnant, not with just one baby, but you are having twins!" Leaving the doctor's office, the first person I called was my husband at that time, Peter Holloway. We were so excited after receiving the good news about being pregnant with twins!

I had already made plans and a reservation to travel on a long distance trip by Greyhound bus. I called my doctor to ask him would it be ok for me to take a long distance trip at this time, being seven weeks pregnant. The doctor reassured me that I would be ok. When it was time to leave, we packed and left. On the day after our arrival at our destination, I began to bleed spots of blood. I was so afraid and concerned of what I thought might be happening at that time. I was running to the phone to call my doctor back home immediately. I informed him of what was going on with me. His response was for me to stay off my feet and keep my legs elevated up. I followed the doctor instructions for the whole seven days I was there. Unfortunately, during that time I suffered a miscarriage. It left me feeling so deeply saddened and depressed for about four months. After that time passed, I was pregnant again and had a beautiful baby girl. I named her after my sister, Zerlene. My daughter was born in 1978. As years came and went, it would happen that one night in a dream, I saw my twin babies again. They were so small I couldn't tell their genders. Long after that first dream, in another dream I saw my twin babies and the only thing they had on was white diapers. I dreamed again about them but this time I knew their genders, two girls dressed in pink clothing with pink sweaters, pink and white dresses, and white ties with white shoes. Also they had lots of thick curly hair. They looked to be about eight months old. When they saw me, they knew who I was. They crawled over to me and climbed up onto my lap, with lots of hugs and kisses. Sometime later during the dream, I remember asking God, "Are these my twin babies that I lost due to the miscarriage?" God answered and said, "Yes, these are they!! Your twin babies." That morning I remember feeling happy and sad at the same time.

In the month of December 2019, I began to have multiple dreams, and during the time that these dreams occurred, I would see small children, sometime babies, mothers, and friends in their homes. This has never failed, that during the dreams there would be a woman I know who would announce that she was pregnant. After awaking from each dream, I began to think about everything I saw in each dream. I was listening to hear God explain the dreams to me. Sometime God speaks immediately but sometimes He chooses to speak later. No matter what He would always instruct me how to proceed. That is why waiting on God is so important. I received a text on March 19th from one of my family members informing me she was pregnant, which was my first confirmation. Then there was a call on April 3, from a friend of the family to tell me that her daughter was pregnant, a second confirmation. God has many ways to speak to his people whether that be through vision, dream, or trance.

From my experience, when dreaming about snakes, the meaning is that an enemy is trying to harm you but is unsuccessful. In my truth, every time I dream and a snake or multiple snakes appear near or far there is an enemy engaged with me. One night while on the phone speaking to a sister of my church, during the conversation we began to disagree about a certain topic. She was getting very frustrated with me as the conversation continued while I remained calm. She went on to share how she truly felt about me and what she had been saying behind my back to other members in the church. I had no idea that she felt this way about me. She proceeded to say, "You think you're so pretty. Everyone always talking about how beautiful you are and how nice you are. Saying all these good things about you. And I would say to them, I disagree with you, she is not pretty, she walk around with her head up in the air, thinking she better than anybody else." I knew then she was my enemy. The conversation ended when I hung up the phone after saying goodbye to her. We didn't speak again for the next few weeks.

There's a saying that goes, "keep your friends close and your enemies closer." The bible is full of similar references. Think about passages like this one. "Love your enemies, do good to those who hate you, bless those who curse you, pray for those who mistreat you. To the one strikes you on the cheek, offer the other also. From one who takes away your cloak do not withhold your tunic either. Give to everyone who ask of you, and from one who takes away your goods do not demand them back. And as you wish that others would do to you, do so to them. Listen, For if you Love them which Love you, what thank have you? for sinners also Love those that Love them. And if you do good to those who do good to you, what benefit is that to you? For even sinners do the same. And if you lend to those from whom you expect to receive, what credit is that to you? Even sinners lend to sinners, to get back the same amount. But Love your enemies, and do good, and lend, expecting nothing in return, and your reward will be great, and you will be children of the Most High, for he is kind to the ungrateful and the evil. Be merciful, even as your Father is merciful." (Luke 6:27-36).

I found out for myself that being an ambassador of God is being someone who is the apple of His eye. You can see Him in the earth everywhere you look. You may ask who God is. For He is the Creator who created both heaven and earth. God want us to see Him, not just in the Spirit, but in everything He created. In the book of Genesis 1:1-31; 2:1-25 it gives us a deeper insight of who God is in the earth. God gave Moses insight and revelation of what happened in the beginning. Not only did Moses hear the word of God spoken to him, Moses saw what happened through revelation. Let's take a look at that revelation.

In the beginning God created the heaven and the earth. And the earth was without form, and void; and darkness was upon the face of the deep. And the Spirit of God moved upon the face of the waters. And God said, Let there be light: and there was light. And God saw the light, that it was good: and God divided the light from the darkness he called Night. And the evening and the morning were the first day. And God said, Let there be a firmament in the midst of the waters, and let it divide the waters from the waters. And God made the firmament, and divided the waters which were under the firmament from the waters which were above the firmament: and it was so. And God called the firmament Heaven. And the evening and the morning were the second day. Then God said,

Let the waters beneath the sky flow together into one place, so dry ground may appear. And that is what happened. God called the dry ground land and the waters seas. And God saw that it was good. Then God said, let the land sprout with vegetation every sort of seed-bearing plant. and trees that grow sees-bearing fruit. These seeds will then produce the kinds of plants and trees from which they came. And that is what happened. The land produced vegetation- all sorts of seed-bearing fruit. Their seeds produced plants and trees of the same kind. And God saw that it was good. And evening passed and morning came, marking the third day.

Then God said, let lights appear in the sky to separate the day from the night. Let them be signs to mark the seasons, days, and years. Let these lights in the sky shine down on the earth. And that is what happened. God made two great lights-the larger one to govern the day, and the smaller one to govern the night. He also made the stars. God set these lights in the sky to light the earth, to govern the day and night, and to separate the light from the darkness. And God saw that it was good. And evening passed and morning came, marking the fourth day. Then God said, Let the waters swarm with fish and other life. Let the skies be filled with birds of every kind. So God created great sea creatures and every living thing that scurries and swarms in the water, and every sort of bird-each producing off-spring of the same kind. And God blessed them, saying, Be fruitful and multiply. Let the fish fill the seas, and let the birds multiply on the earth. And evening passed and morning came, marking the fifth day.

And God said, Let the earth bring forth living souls after their kind, cattle, and creeping thing, and beast of the earth, after their kind. And it was so. And God made the beast of the earth after its kind, and every creeping thing of the ground after its kind. Can you see God everywhere you look yet?!!!!! And God saw that it was good. And God said, Let us make man in our image, after our likeness; and let them have dominion over the fish of the sea, and over the fowl of the heavens, and over the cattle, and over the whole earth, and over every creeping thing that creeps on the earth. So God created human beings in his own image. In the image of God he created them; male and female he created them. Then God blessed them and said, Be fruitful and multiply. Fill the earth and govern it. Reign over the fish in the sea, the birds in the sky, and all the animals that scurry along the ground. Then God said, look I have given you every seed-bearing plant throughout the earth and all the fruit trees for your food. And I have given every green plant as food for all the wild animals, the birds in the sky, and the small animals that scurry along the ground everything that has life. **And that is what happened.** Then God looked over all He had made, and he saw that it was very good! **Now can you see God everywhere you look?** And evening passed and morning came, marking the sixth day.

Let's move on to see more of God in His New Creation. So the creation of the heavens and the earth and everything in them was completed. On the seventh day God had finished his work of creation, so he rested from all his work. And God blessed the seventh day and declared it holy, because it was the day when he rested from all his work of creation. This is the account of the creation of the heavens and the earth. When the Lord God made the earth and the heavens, neither wild plants nor grains were growing on the earth. For the Lord God had not yet sent rain to water the earth, and there were no people to cultivate the soil. Instead, springs came up from the ground and watered all the land. Then the Lord formed the man from the dust of the ground. He breathed the breath of life into the man's nostrils, and the man became a living person.

Then the Lord God planted a garden in Eden in the east, and there he placed the man he had made. The Lord God made all sorts of trees grow up from the ground trees that were beautiful and that produced delicious fruit. In the middle of the garden he placed the tree of life and the tree of the knowledge of good and evil. A river flowed from the land of Eden, watering the garden and then dividing into four branches. The first branch, called the Pishin, flowed around the entire land of Havilah, where gold is found. The gold of that land is exceptionally pure; aromatic resin and onyx stone are also found there. The second branch, called the Gihon, flowed around the entire land of Cush. The third branch, called the Tigris, flowed east of the land of Asshur. The fourth branch is called the Euphrates.

The Lord God placed the man in the Garden of Eden to tend and watch over it. But the Lord God warned him, You may freely eat the fruit of every tree in the garden except the tree of the knowledge of good and evil. If you eat its fruit, you are sure to die. Then the Lord God said, It is not good for the man to be alone. I will make a helper who is just right for him. So the Lord God formed from the ground all the wild animals and all the birds of the sky. He brought them to the man to see what he would call them, and the man chose a name for each one. He gave names to all the livestock, all the birds of the sky, and all the wild animals. But still there was no helper just right for him. So the Lord God caused the man to fall into a deep sleep. While the man slept, the Lord God took out one of the man's ribs and closed up the opening. Then the Lord God made a woman from the rib, and he brought her to the man. At last the man exclaimed. This one is bone from my bone, and flesh from my flesh She will be called woman because she was taken from man. This explains why a man leaves his father and mother and is joined to his wife, and the two are united into one. Now the man and his wife were both naked, but they felt no shame.

Romans 1:20 says, "For the invisible things of him from the creation of the world are clearly seen, being understood by the things that are made, even his eternal power and Godhead; so that they are without excuse: Because that, when they knew God, they glorified him not as God, neither were thankful; but became vain in their imaginations, and their foolish heart was darkened." In the book of Genesis, God -saw- seven times, God -said- ten times, God - called- five times. God saw all these thing first in the spirit then He called them forth.

On November 8, 1997, I saw Jesus high and lifted it up in the sky. He appeared before my eyes. He looked so big in the sky, dressed in all white. It reminded me of a snowy white cloud. In 1997, one day I was in my bedroom kneeling beside my bed praying, suddenly I had a vision, a Man dressed in long white linen garment with a stick in his hand. His hair was long and I even noticed the texture of his hair, it was like wool. I was very curious of who he was, so I asked God who was this man. He answer, "It is Moses." God continued, "I am taking you on a journey where you will see so much more as we enter the 10th heaven, where I am!! You will spend 14 days with me in the spirit realm and when it is time I will send you back." Before that happened, God begin to share his plan concerning my purpose on earth when I return. Then he said, "Keep your eyes on me, I will show you things you never seen, and take you places you have never been before in me." As God was still speaking, in my mind I started to think about the places God had already shown me.

God showed me the beginning of time, the present, and the end of time. Yes!! Past, present, and future. I saw the end of time on earth. In the month of December, in the year 2020, one night after laying my head on my pillow, I begin to dream and what I saw frightened me to my core. There was complete darkness covering whole earth. So much so you could not see your hand in front of your face. As I looked again, I saw through my spiritual eyes a dim light. There were very few people there, those that were there were sitting at tables and on the ground. The people seemed to know they could not go any further. As frightening as it was, I was tempted to keep walking straight into the darkness. Right before taking my last step, I heard a soft, steely voice say, "Stop! Don't go any farther! If you take that last step you will enter into eternal darkness. There is no return from the earth's end." When I woke up, I heard a soft voice explaining the dream saying it was the end of earth. I was shaken, realizing that I had walked to the end of earth.

Another time when in a vision, I looked off to the side and there was a reflection of a pool of water. A bright light shaped in the form of a human being was glowing on the surface of the water. As I continued to look around, I could see beautiful green plants and large fruit trees. The grass was so green it was sparkling like glitter. Nearby was a large lake with crystal clear water. On the banks of the lake there stood a man, dressed in white garment. He was a figure of God who said, "Come follow me." I believed this man to be God, so I followed Him all the way to the palace. My eyes fixed on and were entranced by all of the different angels that was there. I saw at least 100 angels of all shapes and different sizes. Eye-to-eye and face-to-face, God saw my soul was concerned and I had questions. He didn't address any of my concerns, His comfort and presence reassured me not to worry. He said, "You're just passing through." He, along with two angels, continued to lead me through the palace. I remember feeling tired, but I said to myself I've come too far to go back now. As we approach the end of the past, I saw all kinds of things flying around in midair like flying angels and insects crawling on the ground. All of a sudden my desire increased to see Jesus. I begin to say out loud, "I want to see Him!" After repeating those words over and over again, I heard Jesus' voice saying, "Go Back! It's not your time yet, you can't come any farther!"

I turned around and there He was hanging in midair, dressed in white, hovering over me. I could see His face in a form of a cloud so clearly, but when I looked again there was a shekinah Glory cloud. Shekinah is the English transliteration of a Hebrew word meaning, dwelling or settling, the divine presence of God. As He was lifted up high above me, the whole sky was filled with so much pure Light. After seeing the Glory of God, a rainbow appeared in the sky hovering over my head. Rainbows generally mean a symbol of hope and promise as described in Genesis 9:13. God said, "Remember my covenant between me and you and all living creatures of every kind. Never again will the waters become a flood to destroy all life. Whenever the rainbow appears in the clouds, I will see it and remember the everlasting covenant between God and all living creatures of every kind on the earth."

Then I saw a white building. It looked like a city that was so lit up, because the Glory of the Lord again was everywhere. My body began to descend from the vision. I say descend using its literal meaning: To go or pass from a higher to a lower place; move-up or go down. When I opened my eyes, I immediately realized that I was back in my bedroom. Tears begin to flow down my cheek, not wanting to come back to this place called earth. I wanted to stay with God, but that was not His will for me.

So the very next day, during my morning prayers, in a vision, I saw a shadow or an outline of Jesus' face. He could see that I was very concerned. I begin to speak to the Lord about His people, crying uncontrollably. John 11:35 says, "Jesus cried" and my heart was filled with so much compassion for Him and I could see the compassion in His eyes also for me. "Don't cry Lord," I said to Him, being able to feel what He was feeling concerning His people. The bible tells us in Isaiah 55:8 that to understand this scripture, we must first understand who's speaking, then what He's saying, and finally who He is speaking to. When God says to Isaiah, "For my thoughts are not your thoughts, neither are your way my ways, saith the Lord," there was no way Isaiah could understand spiritual things because He was not spirit filled with the Holy Spirit. Once you are born again and filled with the Holy Spirit only then you can understand spiritual things, because you now have access to the mind of God.

1 Corinthians 2:14-16 says, "But the natural man received not the things of the Spirit of God: for they are foolishness unto Him. Neither can He know (them) because they are spiritually discerned." Philippians.2:5 reads, "let this mind be in you, which was also in Christ Jesus." I would like to continue sharing about when I saw God's face. I was in a vision, looking up and there he was, standing in all His gloriousness. He was dressed in white and purple garments, standing on a tall mountain called Mount Zion. The whole mountain was lifted up and I could feel the anointing from God so strongly. Out of His

mouth God spoke these words, "No man can see me and live!" This means with your natural eye, but only in the spirit can you see Him and live, and only then if God allows you to see Him in the spirit. "Behold He is coming with the clouds, and every eye will see Him, even those who pierced Him; and all the kindreds of the earth will mourn over Him." (Revelation 1:7). "Beloved, now are we children of God, and it doth not yet appear what we shall be: but we know that, when He shall appear, we shall be like Him; for we shall see Him as He is." (1 John 3:2). The very next morning in prayer I saw Jesus with stretched out hands saying "Come and follow me," so I did. I looked around and I realized that I was in a strange place, it looked like a cage. Then we begin to ascend upwards on a very high mountain that overlooked everything as far as I could see. I saw beautiful lands of green grass, glistening with a sparking light.

During one of my 40 days and 40 nights consecrations, I experiencing a vision of God dressed in all white with a dozen of yellow and white long stem roses in his hand. He approached me with His hands out to present me with these roses. I felt so honored to receive such a beautiful gift from God! Later in the evening, I was standing in my bedroom near my bed when I saw God in a open vision. Remember an open vision is when your eyes are open and God is showing you things of the past, present, or future. During this open vision, I heard this soft, steeled voice say, "I AM HERE!" I remember falling to my knees because I couldn't stand in His presence. He was standing tall, dressed in a white and purple garment. I've come to realize that each time God shows up, there's always a purpose, whether it be to instruct, correct, or to prepare you by showing you future things to come.

Another type of dream you might experience is a visitation dream. A visitation dream is when someone who has died pays you a visit in a dream. The first time I experienced one of these, I thought I was crazy. I never wondered about or prayed to God to speak to the dead. Even so, I've experienced the dead speaking to me ever since I was about 11 or 12 years old. That is when the dead begin to visit me in my dreams. They began to come more frequently in my 30s. This is perfectly normal, but it is not something I talk about often. When a family member, friend, or acquaintance who has passed on communicates with you in a dream, they usually have a message for a family member or a friend.

There was a man name Mr. George, who I knew. Mr. George was a deacon at my church. He worked for a used car dealership as a salesman. Late one Friday evening, the dealership he worked for was robbed by three men at gun point. As they approached the building, deacon George and the other salesman saw them coming with guns. When he ran toward the door to lock it, they opened fire on him, killing him immediately and injuring others. Five months later, I had a visit from Mr. George in a visitation dream with a message to his dear wife. He asked me to tell her that he made it in. He also asked me to relay to her for her to not worry about him because he was happy now at home.

In another dream, I received a visitation warning message. This was a warning message to me, about two people and their families. I heard the voice of the Lord instruct me to do warfare in the spirit. In the dream, I discerned that their lives were in danger. I could feel the presence of the death Angel close by. My spirit traveled to Tennessee to stop the death Angel from taking this person's life. Then my attention and focus were turned toward another place in Tennessee. I proceeded in the spirit to go there to try and stop the death Angel from taking another life. It was about 10:00 p.m. that night. It turned out that I was too late, the second person was gone. After waking up from the dream, the next day, early that morning I made a phone call to someone I knew who lived in that second region of Tennessee. I began to share with her about the dream I had that night and about what I saw. She verified what I saw. "Yes," she said, "about 10:00 p.m. last night, he passed away." She even said, "I don't know how you knew about what happened. God had to show you."

The Bible says in 2 Corinthians 5:8, "absent from the body, and to be present with the Lord," which means, while we are in this physical life, once we die and become absent from the body of the church in the physical, we pass out of this world and into the eternal life in His Kingdom that He has promised. I have had many different visitation dreams in my life. An operator, in the world of exchanging messages through visitation dreams, this type of dream has happened to me multiple times, for many years.

I did say that I don't like to talk about these visitation dreams, but a close, personal example comes to mind. A very close friend of my family was taken to the hospital. Three days later they passed away due to complications. At that time I was living in Dayton, Ohio and the family friend lived in Indiana, the next state over. My church was in a three day revival. I decided to go to church service that Thursday night. We had a guest speaker, Recharges Blakely. He began to prophesy, calling me to come to front of the church. He proceeded to tell me, "She's already gone." Rev. Blakely asked me to come back tomorrow for the last night of service, and out of obedience, I did. Rev. Blakely after church service was over, turned to me and said, "Be strong." Then I felt a urgency to be by my friend's bedside. I left that night after service to go to the hospital. As I arrived at the hospital, I went straight upstairs to the floor where my friend was. I walked in her room and sat by the side of her bed. It was as the prophet had said, she was gone! I found out that the Doctors had already informed the family she was brain dead, but was waiting for them to accept the report. I couldn't leave, so I stayed there all night, just sitting by her bed. It was about 3:00 a.m. that morning when I was shaken out of my sleep by a disembodied voice calling me by my name. It was her voice. I could hear her voice in my ear, repeating my name over and over again, until she got my attention. This was an inner vision because my eyes were closed but I wasn't asleep. I heard her say, "Tell my children, I won't be back, and get right with God." I also heard, "Tell them the only way they're going to make Heaven their eternal rest, is to give their life completely over to God." This was a warning message from beyond the grave. I asked her, "Where are you?" and the answer I heard in my spirit was, "I don't know where I am, but where I am, it is cold and dark here and my soul is being tormented."

There is a story in Luke 16:19-24. There once was a certain rich man, which was clothed in purple and fine linen, and fared sumptuously every day. A poor man named Lazarus, covered with sores, had been dumped on his doorstep. All he lived for was to get a meal from scraps off the rich man's table. Moreover the dogs who came and licked his sores. Then he died, this poor man, was taken up by the angels to the bosom of Abraham. The rich man also died and was buried. In hell he lifted up his eyes being in torment, he looked up and saw Abraham in the distance and Lazarus in his bosom. He called out, Father Abraham, mercy!! Have mercy!! Send Lazarus to dip his finger in water to cool my tongue. For I am tormented in this flame. But Abraham said, Child, remember that in your lifetime you got the good things and Lazarus the bad things. It's not like that here. Here he's consoled and you're tormented. Besides, in all these matters there is a huge chasm set between us so that no one can go from us to you even if he wanted to, nor can anyone cross over from you to us. The rich man said, Then let me ask you. Father: Send him to the house of my father where I have five brothers, so he can tell them the score and warn them so they won't end up here in this place of torment. Abraham answered, They have Moses and the Prophets to tell them the score. Let them listen to them. I know, Father Abraham, he said but they're not listening. If someone came back to them from the dead, they would change their ways. Abraham replied, If they won't listen to Moses and the prophets they're won't listen to him.

After I was sitting by her bedside all night, the family arrived in the morning. Once again, the Doctor informed the family that she had no brain activity. I left the hospital and went straight to my sister's house, took a shower, and laid down to sleep. I woke up later that evening, got dressed, and went back to the hospital hoping to see her children there. When I arrived only three of them were still there. I asked them to meet me in the waiting room alone. As I begin to share with them what their mother's spirit shared concerning their lives, I relayed the message that I had been given. "She told me to tell you, I won't be back!!!! Tell them to get their life right with God. It's the only way they are going to make it Into the eternal heaven." While relaying this warning message to them, they begin to cry so strongly and react with anger in their voices. The two younger sisters shouted out, "Stop!!! We don't believe you!!" They were in so much grief and denial to the point of refusing to accept the doctor's report. I decided to leave the room. As I left, the oldest sister stopped me to say, "Thank you for sharing our mother's warning." She reassured me that she believed me and for me to not worry.

Two days later, they were planning her funeral. When everything was over, I spoke with the other siblings. I was able to see later how her warning message began to manifest in each one of their lives. I watched their lives change over the years. One of her sons didn't believe there was a God. Now he lives his life as a believer, steadfast in his belief that there is a God. Hallelujah!! The remaining children, their lives are continually changing for the better and as they grow older hopefully they will grow closer and closer to God.

Even with her message delivered, my friend's visitations didn't stop. She would come often to visit me in my dreams, so often that I couldn't tell if it was real or just a dream. In my dreams even though she was deceased, she often would come and sit among us in a room where we would gather. She would sit very quietly off in a corner to herself and as I scanned the room our eyes would meet. The big questions always on my mind were "WHAT ARE YOU DOING HERE?" "WHY ARE YOU HERE? YOU'RE DECEASED." She responded with a smile, nothing more. No one in the room could see her but me. After that, the dreams and visitations would frequently happen. One night after falling asleep, I begin to dream. In the dream, I went to her house where she used to live. The door was open, so I walked in and there she was being a housewife and attending to her children. Observing what I saw, she acknowledged my presence and said, "Come in." I decided to no longer ask the question "Why are you here?", I just accepted her presence and the dreams continued. Closing my eyes I would dream about her and this would happen quite often, so often that it began feeling normal, as though she had come back to life and resumed her old life here on earth.

I was experiencing a series of dreams about her, and the next night was no different. I went into her house again. This time the phone rang and she answered it. The person on the other end started to inform her about two of her oldest daughters and it wasn't good news. We ran as fast as we could down the street, as I thought to myself she's not here in person this is only a familiar spirt. Immediately as I realized I was in a dream, the dream began to fade away and I woke up. A week later I had another dream, but there was something different about this dream than all the other ones. This time when I saw her in my dream, she existed in midair in the midst of a big round circle of light wearing a long green dress. She even looked younger and very beautiful sitting there in a circle of light so bright that it almost blinded me. I kept calling out to her by her name, and she looked straight at me with a big smile on her face. Now I understand about all the times I've seen her in my dreams.

Sometimes God uses people to interpret dreams, like God used Daniel in the bible to interpret Nebuchadnezzar's dreams. God began to show Nebuchadnezzar things to come concerning his future in the form of two dreams. The first dream God answered Daniel in a night vision. Daniel blessed the God of heaven, saying, "Blessed be the name of God, forever and ever. He knows all, does all. He changes the seasons and guides history, He raises up kings and also brings them down, he provides both intelligence and discernment, He opens up the depths, tells secrets, sees in the dark light spills out of him God of all my ancestors, all thanks all praise You made me wise and strong. And now you've shown us what we asked for."

God will let you in on heaven's mysteries, glimpses and sometimes complete pictures of what is coming in the days ahead. The revealer of Mysteries can show you what will happen. But the interpretation is given through whom God pleases, so that you will know and understand what you dreamed and what it means. "When Daniel finished, King Nebuchadnezzar fell on his face in awe before Daniel. He ordered the offering of sacrifices and burning of incense in Daniel's honor. He said to Daniel, Your God is beyond question the God of all gods, the Master of all kings. Your God solves all mysteries, I know, because you've solved this mystery."

Nebuchadnezzar had a second dream. One day while at home taking it easy in his palace without a care in the world. Stretched out on his bed, he had a dream which made him so afraid, he sent for all the wise men in Babylon hoping that they may interpret his dream. These were men of darkness. Magicians, Enchanters, Fortune tellers, Witches. He told them the dream. None could tell him what it meant. Because it was spiritual, which meant it needed a spiritual interpretation. God gave Daniel the ability to interpret dreams and visions. Daniel was a man full of the divine Holy Spirit. Daniel came in, Nebuchadnezzar told him the dream, and then Daniel gave interpretation to it for him. God was warning Nebuchadnezzar about how he was abusing his authority as king. He chose not to ignore Daniel's interpretation concerning the dream. That very hour the dream was fulfilled, for seven years. At the end of the seven years, Nebuchadnezzar looked to heaven and he was given his mind back and he blessed the most high God, thanking and glorifying God, who lives forever. King Nebuchadnezzar learned that he was not God."

Going back to that wonderful day where I had an awesome inner-vision experience with God, I was at the end of the 40 days of consecration. Remembering how I didn't want to leave His presence, I wanted to stay forever but He wouldn't allow it to be so. He instructed me on the things concerning me and what He wanted me to do. I was to lay hands on the sick and the oppressed. He would heal them all. God knew I would obey Him. After coming out of consecration that Saturday night, I would be the first partaker of his will. My chest and back begin to hurt, I cried out to God immediately, and He healed me. God has always healed me. One Sunday morning during Sunday service, my Pastor called me to lay hands on a sick lady. I laid my hands on her stomach, and she began to scream, "It feels like fire burning in my stomach!" I didn't know at that time but found out later she had been diagnosed with stomach cancer. When she went to her doctor, he informed her that she no longer had cancer, anywhere in her body. To God be the Glory!!

Even now the work still continues. I am still laying hands on the sick and they are immediately healed or within that same hour. Let us not forget, Jesus is the healer! Sometimes God would have me send His Word and He healed them not through my touch, but through his Word alone. Similar to the account in Matthew 8:5-13, "When Jesus had entered the village of Capernaum, a Roman captain came to Him in a panic and said, Master, my servant is lying at home sick of the palsy, He can't walk. He's in terrible pain. Jesus said, I'll come and heal him. Oh no, said the captain. I don't want to put you to all that trouble, If you Just speak the Word only, and my servant shall be healed, and immediately his servant was healed." Another example of Jesus healing from afar by His words. At the request of someone whose loved one was suffering, Jesus decided to go to Tire and Sidon House. Before He could get there, a woman of Canaan came down from the hills and pleaded, Master, Have mercy on me. Son of David!!!! "My daughter is severely afflicted by demon-possessed. Jesus ignored her. Then the woman came back to Jesus, and fell to her knees, and begged. Master, help me. But He answered and said, "It's not right to take bread out of the children's mouths and throw it to dogs. She said, You're right, Master, yet even the little dogs eat the crumbs which fall from their masters table. Jesus gave in. O woman, great is your faith!!! Let it be to you as you desire." And right then her daughter was healed from that very hour (Matthew15:21-28). (Mark 7:24-30).

There are a number of mighty miracle examples of Jesus healing people from afar. "There was an official from the king's court whose son was sick. When he heard that Jesus had come out of Judea into Galilee, he went to Him and implored Him to come down and heal his son, for he was at the point of death. Jesus put him off. He rebuked him saying Unless you people see signs and wonders, you will by no means believe. The nobleman said to him, Sir, come down before my child dies. Jesus simply replied, Go your way; your son lives. So the man believed the word that Jesus spoke to him and headed home." (John 4:46-54).

I am here to tell you that I SAW HIM! Not only did I see God spiritually, but I saw him naturally. Just look around and you can see God everywhere! The sun, moon, and stars, God called them forth. In the beginning God created heaven and earth, all you see, all you don't see. When you see the light it represent day, the dark it represent night. These things God called into existence. The sky and water, He divided the waters and made sky. God called forth the earth to bring forth grass, the herb that yields seed, and fruit tree that yields fruit according to its kind, every tree produces seeds of his own kind. Whose seed is in itself, on the earth and it was so. When you can see the fish, and birds, insects, bats, and flying insects, all came from God. All things were made by him; and without him was not anything made that was made. (John 1:3). You can see God when you see the animals, reptiles, wild animals, cattle, and bugs.

God did something even more extraordinary. He created them godlike male and female in His Image and according to His likeness. (Genesis 2:7, 21-22) "God formed man out of dirt from the ground, and breathed into his nostrils the breath of life; and man became a living beings. God put the Man into a deep sleep. As he slept he removed one of his ribs and replaced it with flesh. God then used the rib that he had taken from the Man to make Woman and present her to the Man." He made them, man and woman, reflecting his nature. Open your eyes, there it is. Every time you look at dirt, remember God created male and female from the dirt, and unto dirt they shall return (Genesis 3:19). "We All end up in the same place (dirt). And to dirt we all return. (Ecclesiastes 3:20). "God showed Enoch all his wisdom and power, throughout all the seven days, how he created all the heavenly and earthly forces and all moving things even down to man. Friday the sixth day God commanded in his wisdom to create man from seven consistencies: one, his flesh from the earth; two, his blood from the dew; three, his eyes from the sun; four, his bones from stone; five, his intelligence from the swiftness of the angels and from cloud; six, his veins and his hair from the grass of the earth; seven, his soul from my breath and from the wind. And I gave him seven natures: to the flesh hearing, the eyes for sight, to the soul smell, the veins for touch, the blood for taste, the bones for endurance, to the intelligence sweetness (enjoyment)." In the Bible humans and animals are going to the same place, the dirt. They both came from it; they will both go back to it. Open your eyes and see God in his word, God is seen through manifestation. Grace is love in manifestation. When we look up at the sky, when we look at the trees and eagles flying we see the manifestation of Genesis chapter 1. The Glory of God is seen in the things that He created. His Love is seen in His being. God is Love! He created us in Love that we should walk in the Love-walk. Open your eyes and see God's Love is an action word. Without action there is no love. 1 Corinthians 13:1-8 says If I speak with human eloquence and angelic ecstasy but don't love, I'm nothing but the creaking of a rusty gate. If I speak God's Word with power, of prophecy, and understand all mysteries and making everything plain as day, and if I have faith that says to a mountain be moved, but I don't love, I'm nothing. If I give everything I own to the poor and even go to the stake to be burned as a martyr, but I don't love, I've gotten nowhere. So, no matter what I say, what I believe, and what I do, I'm bankrupt without love.

Love suffers long and is kind; love does not envy. Love does not parade itself, is not puffed up; does not behave rudely, does not seek its own, is not provoked, thinks no evil; does not rejoice in iniquity, but rejoices in the truth; bears all things, believes all things, hopes all things, endures all things. Love never fails. The works of a good deed, for example, clothing the naked like in the book of Matthew 25:35-40 where God says, "I was hungry and you gave me food, I was thirsty and you gave me drink, I was a stranger and you welcomed me, I was naked and you clothed me, I was sick and you visited me, I was in prison and you came to me. Then the righteous will answer him, saying, Lord, when did we see you hungry and feed you, or thirsty and give you drink? And when did we see you a stranger and welcome you, or naked and clothe you? And when did we see you sick or in prison and visit you? And the King will answer them, Truly, I say to you, as you did it to one of the least of these my brothers, you did it to me."

I SAW GOD face to face in the spiritual realm. God had no physical eyes, no physical face and neither did I. The bible says in 1 John 3:2, "when He shall appear, we shall be like Him; For we shall see Him as He is." It was at those time that I SAW GOD Spirit to Spirit. Being in His presence, I experienced God's peace. Having those experiences, operating in my Dreams, Visions, Trances, Prophecies, and hearing God's audible voice has increased His power in my life. Sometimes when my Spiritual discernment meets a person or I pray for a church or a ministry, my spirit will show me things concerning them of which I have no natural Knowledge. My character in this ministry is having a zeal for church purity and a deep sensitivity to evil and the capacity to identify, define, and hate unrighteousness. I am aware of a keen understanding of the danger of false Apostles, Prophets, Evangelists, Pastors, and Teachers. I am called by God to edification, exhortation, and comfort. At times I have been a seer who foretold the future and exposed sin, proclaimed righteousness, warned of judgment to come, and combatted worldliness and lukewarmness among God people. In this ministry I can expect rejection by many in the churches. A church that reject God's prophets will be a declining church, drifting toward worldliness and the compromise of biblical truth and standards.

THE END.

ABOUT THE AUTHOR

Apostle Helen J. Person was born on January 4, 1955 in Sunflower Mississippi. Her family moved to Muncie, Indiana where she was raised. Apostle Helen was surrounded by successful, well known preachers in her family. They were great role models for her while she was growing up. She was interested in the things of God at an early age. Her mother recognized her spirituality and encouraged her along the way.

Apostle Helen gave her life to Lord at a very young age at St. Paul Baptist Church in West Memphis, Arkansas. She was later Baptized at Good Samaritan Baptist Church in Muncie, Indiana. Apostle Helen was licensed and ordained by Bishop George R. Scott, pastor of Christ Worldwide Church, in Dayton, Ohio where she faithfully served until God moved her on to other ministries.

One night while having a dream, a Jewish man wearing a black yarmulke (a skull cap) spoke to her and said, "God has called you to the Nations as an Apostle." On May 5, 2012 she was ordained as an Apostle by Apostle George W. Jobe, Founder of Heaven On Earth International Ministries.

Apostle Helen graduated from High School at the age of seventeen. From there, she attended Grace Ministries Bible College, where she received her degree in Theology. Apostle Helen believes that God has commissioned her to teach the people of God who they are in Christ Jesus and help them in the transition from the Old Man to the New Man. Apostle Helen's statement of Faith is, " The Spirit Of The Lord is upon me. He has anointed me to continue the Ministry of Jesus Christ: preaching, teaching, praying for the sick, raising the dead, proclaiming liberty to captives, recovery of sight to the blind, and to set at liberty those who are oppressed."

Apostle Helen formally Pastored New Birth Christian Fellowship Church in Toledo, Ohio with her husband Pastor Ronald D. Person, under the Spiritual Covering of Apostle Jerry M. Williams, Founder of International Covenant Connections in Raleigh, North Carolina. Apostle Helen was Founder of New Jerusalem Global Outreach Ministries and is also Now Founder of Helen J. Person Ministries.

Made in the USA
Middletown, DE
17 March 2022

62795753R00080